Vegan Food

IN YOUR

Vitamix®

60 Delicious, Nutrient-Packed Recipes for Everyone's Favorite Blender

Emily von Euw

Bestselling author of *Rawsome Vegan Baking*

PAGE STREET
PUBLISHING CO.

Copyright © 2022 Emily von Euw

First published in 2022 by
Page Street Publishing Co.
27 Congress Street, Suite 1511
Salem, MA 01970
www.pagestreetpublishing.com

Distributed by Macmillan, sales in Canada by The Canadian Manda Group.

26 25 24 23 22   1 2 3 4 5

ISBN-13: 978-1-64567-563-1
ISBN-10: 1-64567-563-7

Library of Congress Control Number: 2021944917

Cover and book design by Meg Baskis for Page Street Publishing Co.
Photography by Emily von Euw

Printed and bound in the United States

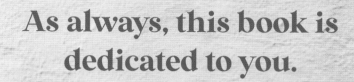

As always, this book is
dedicated to you.

Contents

Introduction

Greetings, salutations, hello and welcome! I'm so glad you're here, friend. We are about to do a lot of blending together.

This book is about combining wholesome plant-based foods with the power of a Vitamix and ending up with delicious vegan, gluten-free recipes. But it's also more than that. I wrote this book with the intention of bringing all my different food-based passions together, and I hope you can feel that! I am passionate about food because it reminds me to be curious, creative, adventurous, patient and in touch with my body, mind and spirit. Food connects us to each other and our planet. In these pages, you're going to find recipes that are accessible and fun to make, recipes that you and your whole family can enjoy and recipes that might just make you see the versatility of fruits and vegetables in a totally new light.

Simply put, this is more than just a smoothie cookbook.

Yes, there is a smoothie chapter, but we are going way beyond that. When you start with a powerful blender and high-quality ingredients, you can make almost anything. The Vitamix is the best blender in the world, by far. I've tried a ton of different high-quality blenders, and none have ever come close to the Vitamix. With this one appliance, we will be creating drinks, snacks, soups, lasagna, quiche, baked treats, sauces, nut butters, plant-based milks and more! Rest assured, the recipes in this book will leave you satisfied and excited to keep exploring what else you can do with your high-speed blender.

My recipes focus on rich flavors and simple ingredients. They are fairly easy and quick to make, but they look and taste more impressive than you'd expect. They are highly nutritious, but you won't feel like you're giving anything up by eating "healthy" dishes. Choosing to make and eat vegan, gluten-free food does not have to feel restrictive or lacking! Whether you eat this way for personal, ethical or health reasons, because you are cooking for someone else who eats plant-based or gluten-free, whether this is a new way of eating for you, or you're already a rock star, everyone can find drinks, snacks, entrees and desserts in here that will tantalize the senses.

More than anything else, I hope these recipes bring you joy.

How to Use This Book

Techniques

I am easygoing when it comes to cooking. I like to go with my gut, follow my intuition and am always open to changing a recipe to suit my own needs and preferences in the moment. Don't worry about following every exact instruction or getting too caught up in measurements and weights. Obviously we need to be specific and calculated to a degree, or else our food will taste weird, get burnt or fall apart. But generally speaking, do what feels right! Environmental differences like humidity and temperature make everyone's kitchen a unique space. Ingredients like flour vary in dryness and grain size. Organics like fruits and vegetables are always slightly different sizes. So no matter what, your recipe will turn out a bit different than mine. That's part of the fun! Feel free to adjust recipes as you see fit. Maybe that means adding a little more olive oil. Maybe that means using a little less tomato sauce. Perhaps it means adding fresh rosemary from your garden. You're the chef! If you don't trust yourself in the kitchen, this is a great way to learn how. If you're already a seasoned pro, you know what I'm talkin' about.

Some notes on using the Vitamix:

- You need patience for some recipes. Especially with nut butters, it's gonna seem like the nuts will never get there. But take your time, take breaks to let the blender cool, and you will end up with a magically creamy result.
- To get an evenly blended result, scrape down the sides of the blender with a rubber spatula once or twice. Always turn off your blender before you open it up and scrape down the sides.
- Use the tamper that your Vitamix comes with to keep everything moving. You can use it as you're blending. Rotate it in a circular motion in the direction the blades move.
- When you're ready to clean your Vitamix, add some warm soapy water to the container, put the lid back on and blend for a few seconds! This does most of the hard work for you before you clean everything in the sink. I don't recommend putting your Vitamix in the dishwasher.

Ingredients

I designed these recipes to be *actually* doable for *almost* any kind of cook, so most of the ingredients will be familiar and readily available. There might be one or two that you haven't heard of or used yet. In those cases, they will be available at your local health food store or online.

We will be using a variety of colorful fruits, vegetables, tofu, nuts, seeds and beans. I love rich flavors, so we will be incorporating lots of herbs and spices, too. This is a gluten-free cookbook, so the grains we use will be gluten-free pastas, flours and rices. If you don't need to eat gluten-free, you can of course substitute gluten-full ingredients instead! As always: do what works best for you.

I always recommend finding the freshest produce (preferably organic and local) and the highest-quality dry goods available. Farmers markets, organic grocery shops and artisan food stores are excellent places to find the best quality ingredients. However, quality often costs more, and so if the $30 bottle of organic, unfiltered award-winning olive oil is not in your budget, no sweat. Get what you can afford!

Tip: If you're shopping on a budget or don't have access to organic, local produce, go for frozen fruits and veggies. They're usually cheaper pound for pound, *and* they're fresher than some conventional produce in the grocery store because they're picked when they're actually ripe. A lot of conventional produce we see in the grocery store is picked weeks or months before it naturally ripens. This makes for less-flavorful produce because the starches can't develop into sugars under the sun and directly from the tree or bush.

If you do feel like splurging on some specialty items, there are a few I would specifically recommend:

- Maldon salt: a wonderful flaked salt perfect for finishing any savory dish
- Smoked paprika powder: adds a rich, complex flavor punch to every meal
- Good olive oil: look for ones in a dark glass bottle labeled 100% pure extra-virgin olive oil
- Maple syrup: it's my favorite sweetener, and I'm gonna be honest, I will drink spoonfuls of the stuff straight from the container

Leftovers

In my opinion, leftovers are a holy food. I can't even count the number of times I've staggered into the kitchen praying for a miracle of food to manifest because I simply cannot be bothered to cook that day. I open the fridge and *angelic music* there's the fettuccine I forgot I made two days ago! Add some Maldon salt on top, a sprinkle of fresh basil, a drizzle of olive oil, and I've got a five-star meal straight from heaven.

For this book, having leftovers of certain recipes will come in handy when you want to try other recipes. Most of the recipes in Vitamixed Mains (page 35) require recipes from Basic Blends (page 119), Easy Sauces, Dips and Spreads (page 93) and Creamy Dreamy Soups (page 23). So, if you're looking to save time, it will work to your advantage to make recipes from the Basic Blends earlier in the week to snack on, and then use those leftovers for Vitamixed Mains recipes later on. For example, you feel like trying out the Basil Arugula Pesto with Walnuts (page 97) on Tuesday, and you have it with some crackers or vegetables. Later that week, if you want to try the Plant-Based Lasagna with Pesto, Mushrooms and Chickpeas (page 52), you've already got the pesto leftovers ready to go! Of course, none of the recipes in here are super complicated or time consuming, but this is just a little cookbook hack I felt was worth sharing.

Superfood Smoothies

It's a Vitamix cookbook, so of course we're gonna start with smoothies. This chapter is a handful of simple, highly nutritious—yet tasty—drinks that are super-quick and easy to make. I like keeping my smoothies pretty basic, so there aren't any recipes in here that have 1,000 ingredients and end up looking and tasting like . . . sludge. We are keeping ingredient lists short and smoothie colors vibrant and beautiful. I really tried to keep every member of the family in mind when I designed these recipes. So from Grandpa to the kiddies, these recipes should please.

The most far-out ingredients in this chapter are spirulina powder (a green superfood) and sea buckthorn berries (super high in vitamin C and kinda taste like candy). Both these items can be found at health food stores or online. Cheers!

Strawberry Vanilla Shake with Banana

YIELD: 2 CUPS (480 ML)

This is a basic fruit smoothie for people who might not normally "like smoothies" (think: kids, smoothie newbies or your brother who refuses to eat fruits or vegetables). This recipe has a creamy texture and a sweet fruity flavor. Strawberries are rich in antioxidants and bananas offer potassium. Vanilla extract and a Medjool date make this taste like a strawberry milkshake!

1 banana (118 g), sliced into 1" (2.5-cm) pieces

1 cup (144 g) sliced frozen strawberries

½ cup (120 ml) almond milk (page 135) or other non-dairy milk

½ tsp vanilla extract

1 Medjool date, pitted

½ tsp lemon juice

Add all of the ingredients to your Vitamix and blend for 30 to 60 seconds, or until smooth, pink and creamy. Enjoy right away!

Berry Apple Smoothie

YIELD: 2½ CUPS (600 ML)

This is a fruit smoothie full of antioxidants, fiber, vitamin C and tart sweetness. Thanks to the apple, this recipe is more on the juicy side instead of the creamy side. Hemp milk adds some protein and a nutty flavor! Blueberries are one of my favorite fruits because the house I grew up in has five blueberry bushes growing in the front yard. Each year, I got to watch them sprout new leaves, blossoms and finally, berries. Each bush produced differently shaped, colored and flavored berries. One bush grew right next to lavender, so its berries always tasted lightly of the flower. Nature is divine!

1 green apple (182 g), peeled and chopped into 1" (2.5-cm) pieces

1 cup (150 g) frozen mixed berries (blueberries, blackberries and raspberries)

½ cup (120 ml) non-dairy milk

1 tsp lime juice

Pinch of stevia powder (optional)

Add all of the ingredients, except the stevia, to your Vitamix and blend for 30 to 60 seconds, or until smooth and evenly purple. Blend in a pinch of stevia if you want a sweeter aftertaste. Enjoy right away!

Daily Greens Smoothie

YIELD: 2½ CUPS (600 ML)

Pretty much everyone agrees that eating more leafy greens is a good idea for a healthy body and mind. But sometimes I don't feel like eating a big salad or a bunch of spinach. So . . . we blend! This smoothie is full of vitamins and minerals thanks to the green superstars: spinach, kale and spirulina.

1 frozen banana (118 g), sliced into 1" (2.5-cm) pieces

1 cup (30 g) spinach

1 cup (67 g) kale

1 cup (240 ml) pure fruit juice (I like a mango and orange blend)

1 tsp lemon juice

½ tsp spirulina powder

1–3 ice cubes (optional)

Add all of the ingredients to your Vitamix and blend for 30 to 60 seconds, or until the greens are thoroughly blended. If you want more of a slushie, blend in 1 to 3 ice cubes. Enjoy right away!

Tropical Fruit Smoothie with Mango and Pineapple

I love tropical fruits! They are always rich in vitamins, antioxidants, color and flavor. There are so many unique and beautiful fruits out there, and learning about new ones is fun and interesting for me. We will keep it relatively familiar with this recipe, though, and blend up two of my favorite gems: mango and pineapple. Mango is an exceptionally sweet and creamy fruit and thus pairs well with the tart juiciness of pineapple. I add a pinch of basil for its refreshing flavor.

1 cup (140 g) frozen mango chunks, thawed

1 cup (165 g) frozen pineapple chunks, thawed

1½ cups (360 ml) coconut milk

Pinch of fresh basil leaves

1 tbsp (15 ml) coconut nectar or maple syrup

1 tbsp (15 ml) lime juice

Pinch of stevia powder (optional)

Add all of the ingredients, except the stevia, to your Vitamix and blend for 30 to 60 seconds, or until smooth. Blend in a pinch of stevia if you want a sweeter aftertaste. Enjoy right away!

Note: I find it simplest to just buy frozen bags of sliced fruits whenever available. Often this allows me to enjoy the freshest possible version, because frozen fruits and veggies are picked when they're ripe (instead of before). Plus, it saves a bunch of time and mess because the fruit is already peeled and sliced. Lastly, it's cheaper!

Sea Buckthorn and Orange Slushie

YIELD: 2 CUPS (480 ML)

Sea buckthorn berries are one of the most delicious berries that most folks haven't heard of. They are super high in vitamin C, taste a little like citrus and a little like candy, but you just have to try them to know what I am talking about! Here we blend them with orange to bring out the citrus flavor, plus a bit of lemon, maple syrup and green apple to bring in some tartness and some sweetness.

½ cup (75 g) frozen sea buckthorn berries

1 orange (160 g), peeled and quartered

½ green apple (90 g), quartered

¼ cup (60 ml) orange juice, plus more if needed

1 tsp maple syrup

1 tsp lemon juice

1–3 ice cubes (optional)

Add all of the ingredients to your Vitamix and blend for 30 to 60 seconds, or until you get a delicious orange fruit slushie. Add more orange juice in ¼-cup (60-ml) increments if it's too thick. If you want it even colder and frostier, blend in 1 to 3 ice cubes. Enjoy right away!

Creamy Dreamy Soups

I don't think it's a bold statement to say soup is one of the most wonderful and universally beloved foods on the planet. It's full of nourishing ingredients, it's endlessly versatile and cost-effective and it's often symbolized as the loving care we give to one another. The Vitamix is a champ at blending perfect, flavorful soups, and that's what this chapter is all about. Since this is also a vegan cookbook, we are going heavy on the vegetables! In each recipe, even though we will be using totally different veggies, herbs and spices, the outcome is always a balance of sweet, salty and savory umami. Depending on your mood, you can blend these soups until totally smooth or leave them a little chunky.

Carrot Coconut Soup with Caramelized Onions

YIELD: 6 CUPS (1.4 L)

When you invest in a Vitamix, you almost won't believe how smooth and creamy your soups will be! One of the many reasons I love my Vitamix is because of how easy it is to make your own exquisite soups at home. They are cost-effective, great for leftovers and an excellent way to maximize the veggies you eat in a day. This creamy, savory soup is full of nutritious ingredients and rich flavor from roasted carrots, caramelized onions and coconut milk.

5 cups (640 g) peeled and chopped carrots (½" [1.3-cm] pieces)

2 cloves garlic (14 g), peeled and minced

½ tsp coriander powder

½ tsp smoked paprika powder

½ tsp turmeric powder

¼ cup (60 ml) extra-virgin olive oil, divided

1 medium Vidalia onion (200 g), sliced

1 tsp sea salt, plus more to taste

¼ tsp cracked black pepper, plus more to taste

½ tsp ginger powder

3 cups (720 ml) vegetable broth or water, plus more if needed

½ cup (120 ml) full-fat coconut milk

1 tsp lemon juice, plus more to taste

Preheat the oven to 400°F (200°C). Line a baking sheet with parchment paper.

In a large bowl, mix together the carrots, garlic, coriander, smoked paprika, turmeric and 2 tablespoons (30 ml) of the olive oil. Roast for 25 minutes, and then check the carrots. You want them to be starting to brown and be soft all the way through. If they need more time, rearrange them in the pan and continue baking for another 10 to 15 minutes, checking periodically until they're done.

While the carrots are cooking, make your caramelized onions. In a saucepan over medium-low heat, add the remaining olive oil and onion. Cover and cook for 15 minutes, occasionally checking on the slices and stirring. Finish cooking, uncovered, over medium heat for 5 minutes, or until they are golden brown.

Add the carrots, onion, salt, pepper, ginger powder, 3 cups (720 ml) of the broth, coconut milk and lemon juice to your Vitamix. Blend until very smooth, adding more broth as needed. Adjust according to taste, adding more salt, pepper, lemon juice or other spices, if desired. Pour into bowls and enjoy right away! This will keep for 1 week in the fridge.

Creamy Broccoli Soup

YIELD: 6 CUPS (1.4 L)

When you don't feel like eating your broccoli . . . turn it into soup! The slow-sautéed onions and garlic bring big savory flavor to this recipe, and a splash of lemon juice brightens it up. I added cashews for creaminess and a subtle, sweet, nutty flavor.

2 tbsp (30 ml) extra-virgin olive oil

3 cloves garlic (21 g), peeled and minced

1 large celery rib (64 g), chopped into 1" (2.5-cm) pieces

1 medium Vidalia onion (200 g), chopped into ½" (1.3-cm) pieces

7 cups (637 g) packed broccoli florets

1 tsp sea salt, plus more to taste

¼ tsp cracked black pepper, plus more to taste

3–4 cups (720–960 ml) vegetable broth or water, divided, plus more if needed

½ cup (73 g) raw cashews

1 tsp lemon juice

Add the oil, garlic, celery and onion to a large pot or pan over medium-low heat. Cook, covered, stirring occasionally for 15 minutes, or until the onion is translucent and tender. Add the broccoli, salt, pepper and ½ cup (120 ml) of the broth. Simmer for 10 minutes, or until the broccoli is vibrant green and softened.

Add the contents of the pot to your Vitamix, along with the remaining broth, cashews and lemon juice. Blend for 1 minute, or until smooth, adding more broth if needed. Adjust according to taste, adding more salt or pepper, if desired. Pour into bowls and enjoy right away! This will keep for 1 week in the fridge.

Butternut Squash Soup with Garden Herbs

YIELD: 6 CUPS (1.4 L)

Squash is one of my favorite foods. It's creamy and sweet and pairs well with so many different things! In my humble opinion, the best way to prepare squash is to roast it with lots of garlic, oil and herbs. We add coconut milk to this recipe to make it an ultra-creamy soup, but if you're craving a lighter soup, just use more vegetable broth instead of coconut milk. The herbs in this recipe—rosemary, thyme and oregano—can be grown on most balconies (or even on a windowsill if you get enough light)! I'm lucky to have a garden where I can harvest many of my herbs.

1 (3-lb [1.4-kg]) butternut squash, halved lengthwise and deseeded

2 tbsp (30 ml) melted coconut oil

1 tsp sea salt, plus more to taste

¼ tsp cracked black pepper, plus more to taste

3 cloves garlic (21 g), peeled and minced

1 tsp fresh rosemary leaves

1 tsp fresh thyme leaves

1 tsp fresh oregano leaves

3 cups (720 ml) vegetable broth or water, plus more if needed

½ cup (120 ml) full-fat coconut milk

Preheat the oven to 375°F (190°C). Line a baking sheet with parchment paper.

Place the butternut squash halves, flesh sides facing up, on the baking sheet. Deeply score the squash and drizzle on the coconut oil. Add the salt, pepper, garlic, rosemary, thyme and oregano on top. Roast for 45 to 60 minutes, or until it's soft all the way through and beginning to brown. Check the squash halfway through baking to see if it's getting too brown. If it is, place a large piece of tinfoil on top of the squash and fold it around the edges so it stays put. Let the squash cool enough so you can handle it. Scoop out the flesh, place in the Vitamix and discard the skins.

Add the broth and coconut milk to the Vitamix. Blend for 1 minute, or until smooth, adding more vegetable broth if needed. Adjust according to taste, adding more salt or pepper as desired. Pour into bowls and enjoy right away! This will keep in the fridge for 1 week.

Roasted Tomato Soup with Sweet Corn and Garlic

YIELD: 5 CUPS (1.2 L)

Tomatoes are one of my favorite vegetables! Er, I mean fruits. (Yes, tomatoes are in fact a fruit.) I adore their sweet and savory flavors, their acidity, their juiciness and their color. They are so versatile, being delicious both raw and cooked. Tomatoes are rich in the antioxidant lycopene, which may help reduce the risk of cancer and heart disease. These beautiful red gems also offer vitamin C, potassium, folate and vitamin K. Most importantly, they taste superb! In this recipe, we are blending roasted tomatoes with sweet corn, garlic and spices for a deliciously smoky, rich soup. This is perfect as it is or as a sauce for linguine or fettuccine.

3 cups (540 g) tomatoes, roughly chopped (preferably organic and local for best flavor!)

1½ cups (231 g) sweet corn

3 cloves garlic (21 g), peeled

2 tbsp (30 ml) extra-virgin olive oil

1 tsp sea salt, plus more to taste

¼ tsp black pepper

1 tbsp (18 g) miso paste, plus more to taste

2 cups (480 ml) vegetable broth or water, plus more if needed

1 tbsp (3 g) chopped fresh basil leaves

1 tbsp (15 ml) balsamic vinegar glaze

Preheat the oven to 500°F (260°C). Line a baking sheet with parchment paper.

Spread the tomatoes, corn and garlic on the baking sheet. Drizzle with the olive oil and sprinkle on the salt and pepper. Bake for 20 minutes, or until everything is starting to get browned on the edges. Remove from the oven and let cool. Reserve 2 tablespoons (30 g) of the roasted veggies for garnishing.

Add the miso paste, vegetable broth and roasted veggies to your Vitamix and blend until smooth. Add extra vegetable broth in ½-cup (120-ml) increments, if needed, until the soup is the consistency you prefer. Taste and adjust accordingly, adding more salt or miso paste, if desired. Garnish with the basil, balsamic glaze and reserved roasted veggies. Enjoy! This will keep in the fridge for 1 week.

Earthy Mushroom Soup with Thyme and Ginger

YIELD: 3 CUPS (720 ML)

There are two kinds of people in this world: those who like mushrooms and those who haven't had mushrooms prepared the right way yet. Okay, so I'm joking a little, but there is some truth to that! I am obviously a mushroom lover, and I do believe I can turn any mushroom avoider into a fan. If it's a texture thing, we can fix that. If it's a flavor thing, we can fix that! I will eat mushrooms in almost any form, and soup is no exception. In this recipe, we are sautéing the 'shrooms for full flavor effect with garlic and herbs, and then blending that with coconut milk and mushroom broth for a super creamy and earthy soup.

2 tbsp (30 ml) extra-virgin olive oil

2 cloves garlic (14 g), peeled and minced

1 tsp peeled and minced fresh ginger root

½ tsp fresh thyme leaves

¼ tsp cracked black pepper

3 cups (225 g) chopped cremini mushrooms

¼ cup (27 g) pecan pieces

½ cup (120 ml) full-fat coconut milk

1 cup (240 ml) mushroom broth, vegetable broth or water, plus more if needed

½ tsp sea salt

1 tsp toasted sesame seeds

1 tsp sesame oil

Warm a large, nonstick saucepan over medium-low heat. Add the oil, garlic, ginger, thyme, pepper and mushrooms. Sauté, covered, while stirring occasionally, for 10 minutes, or until the mixture smells fragrant and the mushrooms are beginning to soften and brown. Reserve 2 tablespoons (9 g) of the mushrooms for garnishing.

Add the sautéed mixture, pecans, coconut milk, broth and salt to your Vitamix, and blend until smooth. Add extra broth as needed. Garnish with the sesame seeds, sesame oil and reserved mushrooms. This will keep for 1 week in the fridge.

Vitamixed Mains

We have arrived at the main feature! The recipes in this chapter are based around other recipes in this book—we are putting together different parts (like soups and sauces) to make a whole, finished product. So, while not every recipe in this chapter needs a Vitamix, the recipes that help make up these main courses do. Each of these mains has a balance of flavor, texture and color. And of course, while they taste rich and satisfying, they also provide a bunch of micronutrients and macronutrients. That's the magic of vegetables, whole grains, beans, seeds, nuts . . . and your Vitamix.

Carrot Coconut Soup with Marinated Tofu and Tamari Almonds

YIELD: 2 LARGE OR 3 REGULAR PORTIONS

This is a big umami meal: Savory and subtle sweetness come together for a rich, earthy flavor profile that will have you enjoying every bite (or spoonful). Coconut milk and carrots are a power couple in the soup, marinated tofu adds another texture (and protein) and the tamari almonds are the perfect crunchy, salty topping.

1 (12.3-oz [349-g]) package extra-firm or medium-firm tofu

1 batch Ginger Tahini Tofu Marinade (page 109)

¼ cup (36 g) slivered almonds

1 tbsp (15 ml) gluten-free tamari

½ tsp sesame oil

4 cups (960 ml) Carrot Coconut Soup with Caramelized Onions (page 24), heated

Slice the tofu into very small ¼-inch (6-mm) cubes. Place the cubed tofu into a large resealable plastic bag or a bowl, and add the marinade. Gently shake so the tofu is entirely coated. Let this sit for as long as possible. (A few days would be great, but 10 to 20 minutes is okay, too!) If you will be marinating the tofu for longer than 1 hour, put it in the fridge. Otherwise, leave it out on your counter while you prepare the rest of the meal.

Sauté the tofu in a large nonstick pan over medium heat for 10 to 15 minutes, or until the marinade has been absorbed and the tofu begins to brown. (Alternatively, you can bake the tofu at 350°F [180°C] for 30 minutes, or until the tofu begins to brown.)

Preheat the oven to 300°F (150°C). Line a baking sheet with parchment paper.

In a bowl, toss the almonds with the tamari and sesame oil. Lay the almonds out on the baking sheet. Bake for 5 to 7 minutes, or until the almonds begin to brown. Keep an eye on them so they don't burn.

Pour the soup into bowls. Gently add the tofu, followed by the tamari almonds. Enjoy right away! If there are leftovers, this will keep in the fridge for 3 to 4 days.

Creamy Broccoli Soup with Sautéed Kale, Pecans and Pesto Penne

YIELD: 3 LARGE OR 4 REGULAR PORTIONS

Green goodness! Leafy greens are one of the most nutrient-dense foods on the planet, and despite what you may have believed growing up (if you were forced to eat boiled or steamed broccoli or Brussels sprouts), they can be cooked into amazing deliciousness. You just need a little oil, salt and heat. Wholesome, simple cooking actually makes you forget you're eating something healthy, because the food just tastes GOOD.

¼ cup (27 g) raw pecan pieces

2 bunches (170 g) kale

1 tbsp (15 ml) melted coconut oil

⅛ tsp sea salt

⅛ tsp cracked black pepper

⅛ tsp garlic powder

2 heaping cups (200 g) uncooked gluten-free penne

½ cup (120 ml) Basil Arugula Pesto with Walnuts (page 97)

4 cups (960 ml) Creamy Broccoli Soup (page 27), heated

Warm a nonstick pan over medium heat. Add the pecans and toast for 2 to 4 minutes, or until they begin to brown and smell very fragrant. Set aside.

Cut the stems off the kale leaves, and cut the leaves into bite-sized pieces. In a large nonstick pan over medium heat, add the kale, coconut oil, salt, pepper and garlic powder. Stir and then cook with the pan covered for 1 to 2 minutes. Uncover and finish cooking the kale for 1 to 2 minutes. The kale is ready when it's softened, vibrant green and tender.

Cook the penne according to the directions on the package. In a large bowl, toss the cooked penne in the pesto.

Pour the hot soup into bowls. Add the pesto penne, and then arrange the sautéed kale on top and sprinkle on the pecans. Enjoy right away! If there are leftovers, this will keep in the fridge for 3 to 4 days.

Roasted Butternut Squash Soup with Brown Rice and Chickpea Salad

YIELD: 2 LARGE OR 3 REGULAR PORTIONS

This is a wonderful, nourishing and colorful meal for entertaining guests on a summer evening. Or just a delicious meal to enjoy any time! If you drink, I'd recommend pairing this with chilled white wine. I try to keep all my meal recipes balanced with micronutrients and macronutrients, and there are many ways to do that beyond the typical and traditional "meat, vegetable, carb" equation. The brown rice and chickpea salad is full of protein but tastes light and fresh thanks to the basil, veggies and tangy dressing. The soup is warming and earthy. A match made in heaven.

2 cups (372 g) cooked short-grain brown rice, cooled

2 cups (328 g) cooked chickpeas

2 cups (60 g) roughly chopped spinach

1 medium tomato (200 g), diced

1 cup (120 g) thinly sliced cucumber

⅔ cup (33 g) finely chopped fresh basil, divided

3 tbsp (45 ml) extra-virgin olive oil, plus more to taste

2 tbsp (30 ml) rice vinegar or balsamic vinegar

1 tsp flaked salt, plus more to taste

¼ tsp garlic powder

4 cups (960 ml) Butternut Squash Soup with Garden Herbs (page 28), heated

¼ cup (27 g) raw or toasted pecan pieces

In a large bowl, toss the rice with the chickpeas. Add the spinach, tomato, cucumber and ½ cup (20 g) of the basil. Add the olive oil, vinegar, salt and garlic powder and toss gently to coat all the ingredients. Have a taste and adjust accordingly. Feel free to add more dressing or some extra olive oil and flaked salt.

Pour the soup into bowls and garnish with the remaining basil. In different bowls, portion out the rice and chickpea salad and garnish with the pecans. Or, you can add it all to one bowl. Enjoy right away! This will keep in the fridge for 3 to 4 days.

Tomato Soup with Garlic Bread and Cranberry Walnut Salad

YIELD: 2 LARGE OR 3 REGULAR PORTIONS

Tomato soup and toast is an ultimate comfort food combo for me. This is an elevated, wholesome version! I highly suggest dipping the bread into the soup as you eat it, so it soaks up the flavor and gets nice and soft. A crunchy, sweet-and-tart side salad balances it all out.

3 tbsp (45 ml) extra-virgin olive oil

2 tbsp (30 ml) balsamic vinegar

1 tsp maple syrup

¼ tsp garlic powder

¼ tsp black pepper

½ tsp Dijon mustard

1 bunch (200 g) curly kale

3 tbsp (42 g) chopped walnuts

3 tbsp (23 g) dried cranberries

4 slices of your favorite gluten-free bread

¼ cup (60 g) Buttery Spread with Herbs and Garlic (page 98)

4 cups (960 ml) Roasted Tomato Soup with Sweet Corn and Garlic (page 31), heated

In a large bowl, whisk together the olive oil, balsamic vinegar, maple syrup, garlic powder, pepper and mustard. Tear the kale leaves off the stems. Coat the leaves in the dressing. I recommend massaging the dressing into the leaves with your hands to soften the greens and really infuse the flavor. Garnish with the chopped walnuts and dried cranberries.

Toast the bread, and then spread on the buttery spread. Pour the soup into bowls, and add your buttered toast on a side plate or the edge of the bowl, alongside the salad. Enjoy right away!

Earthy Mushroom Soup with Soba Noodles, Green Onion and Edamame

YIELD: 2 LARGE OR 3 REGULAR PORTIONS

Soba noodles (made from buckwheat) are naturally gluten-free and so tasty! They also cook way faster than wheat noodles, so if you already have your soup made, this is a really quick recipe to throw together. Edamame (green soybeans) are full of protein and delicious flavor. Like tons of people around the world, I love edamame on its own: steamed and sprinkled with a pinch of salt. Green onions add a crunch for an all-around balanced meal of texture, flavor and color.

4 oz (115 g) gluten-free soba noodles or rice noodles

1 tsp sesame oil

¼ tsp flaked salt (I use Maldon salt)

4 cups (960 ml) Earthy Mushroom Soup with Thyme and Ginger (page 32), heated

½ cup (47 g) steamed edamame

2 tbsp (6 g) thinly sliced green onion

1 tbsp (9 g) raw or toasted sesame seeds

Cook the noodles according to the directions on the package. Once drained, toss the noodles with the sesame oil and salt. Pour the soup into bowls and add the noodles. Finish garnishing with edamame, green onion and sesame seeds. Enjoy right away! This will keep for up to 3 days in the fridge.

Mac and Cheese with Marinated Tempeh and Steamed Broccolini

YIELD: 4 LARGE OR 6 REGULAR PORTIONS

Like many people on this earth, mac and cheese is a huge comfort food of mine. This is a veganized and healthified version, designed to maintain all that big flavor, creamy texture and filling satisfaction while using whole-food ingredients instead of more processed foods. And of course, when you've got your Vitamix, this all comes together easily!

1 (6-oz [225-g]) package plain tempeh

¾ cup (180 ml) BBQ Sauce with Tamarind and Orange (page 106)

3 cups (250 g) uncooked gluten-free macaroni

3 cups (273 g) broccolini*

2 cups (480 ml) Cheesy Sauce (page 113)

¼ cup (36 g) toasted cashews (optional)

* Broccolini is just baby broccoli, so feel free to use regular grown-up broccoli if you can't find broccolini.

Slice the tempeh if it's not already sliced. In a shallow dish, glassware container or resealable plastic bag, add the tempeh slices and the BBQ sauce. If possible, let the tempeh marinate covered in the fridge for a good 24 hours or more. Otherwise, leave the tempeh at room temperature to marinate, covered, while you make the rest of the meal.

Preheat the oven to 375°F (190°C). Line a baking sheet with parchment paper.

Evenly arrange the BBQ tempeh on the baking sheet. Bake for 20 minutes, or until the tempeh is looking caramelized and a much darker brown. Raise the oven temperature to 450°F (230°C), or use your oven's broil feature, and cook for 1 minute.

Cook the macaroni according to the directions on the package.

Cover the bottom of a saucepan with 1 inch (2.5 cm) of water, and bring the water to a boil over high heat. Place a steamer basket inside the pot along with your broccolini. Reduce the heat to medium and steam the broccolini for 3 to 5 minutes, or until it's vibrant green and becoming tender.

Scoop the macaroni into bowls. Add the Cheesy Sauce and gently mix it in. Add the BBQ tempeh, and then arrange the steamed broccolini around the edges. Sprinkle on the toasted cashews, if using, and enjoy!

Crispy Lettuce and Lentil Salad with Creamy Chipotle Dressing

YIELD: 2 LARGE OR 3 REGULAR PORTIONS

I. Love. Salad. I think a lot of folks look down on salad because they don't know how darn delicious it can be. Salad does not just have to be sad, wilted greens with a miniscule amount of oil and vinegar! In this recipe, we top off crispy shredded lettuce with a rich and creamy dressing, protein-rich lentils, crunchy walnuts, fresh avocado and juicy beets.

4 cups (140 g) shredded butter or romaine lettuce

⅓ cup (80 ml) Creamy Dressing with Chipotle and Nutritional Yeast (page 105), or to taste

½ cup (100 g) cooked green or brown lentils

1 avocado (150 g), pitted and cut into ½" (1.3-cm) pieces

1 cooked beet (100 g), sliced into ½" (1.3-cm) pieces

½ cup (59 g) roughly chopped walnuts

1 tsp lemon juice (optional)

In a large bowl, toss the lettuce in the dressing, adding as much or as little dressing as you prefer. Scoop into bowls and add the lentils, avocado, beet and walnuts. Spritz with some lemon juice, if using. Enjoy right away!

Tofu Quiche with Mushrooms, Spinach and Leek

YIELD: 1 (9" [23-CM]) QUICHE OR 8 SERVINGS

This recipe is inspired by an unforgettable quiche I enjoyed at a vegetarian café—
The Coup—in Calgary many years ago. This is one of my favorite recipes
in this book, and it makes a great brunch.

FOR THE QUICHE BATTER

1 (1-lb [454-g]) package medium-firm tofu

¼ cup (20 g) nutritional yeast

2 tbsp (30 ml) extra-virgin olive oil

1 tsp minced garlic

1 tsp black salt or sea salt, plus more to taste

1 tbsp (8 g) gluten-free cornstarch

½ tsp cracked black pepper

½ tsp turmeric powder

½ tsp smoked paprika powder

½ tsp onion powder

FOR THE VEGETABLES

3 tbsp (45 ml) extra-virgin olive oil

3 cloves minced garlic

1 tsp fresh minced ginger

1 cup (75 g) thinly sliced cremini mushrooms

1 cup (90 g) thinly sliced leek

½ cup (90 g) thinly sliced cherry tomatoes

3 cups (90 g) spinach leaves

1 Savory Gluten-Free Tart Crust (page 147)

Preheat the oven to 350°F (180°C).

To make the batter, press or strain the excess water out of the tofu as much as possible. Add all of the quiche batter ingredients to your Vitamix and blend for 10 seconds, or until the mixture is smooth and yellow. Adjust according to taste, adding more spices or salt, if desired. Leave the mixture in the blender container for now.

Now let's prepare the veggies! Add the oil to a large, nonstick pan and turn the heat to medium-high. Once the oil has heated up, add the garlic, ginger and mushrooms. Cook for 5 minutes, stirring occasionally, until the mushrooms start to brown and smell fragrant. Add the leek and continue sautéing for 4 minutes, or until the leek has softened and is beginning to look translucent. Add the tomatoes and sauté for 2 minutes, or until the tomatoes begin to soften and wrinkle. Add the spinach and stir it into the hot vegetables for 1 to 2 minutes, or until the spinach wilts and is vibrant green.

Spoon half of the sautéed vegetables into the crust and arrange them evenly on the bottom. Pour in the quiche batter. Arrange the rest of the vegetables on top. Bake for 40 to 50 minutes, or until the middle of the quiche is firm and doesn't jiggle and the edges of the crust are golden brown. If your crust is looking too dark before the quiche is finished, cover the quiche with tinfoil to protect it from burning. Let it cool completely (an hour or so), and then slice and enjoy! This will keep in the fridge for 1 week.

Plant-Based Lasagna with Pesto, Mushrooms and Chickpeas

YIELD: 1 (9 X 13" [23 X 33-CM]) LASAGNA

Lasagna is one of my favorite big dishes to make. It's a crowd-pleaser . . . and great for leftovers. Pesto is such a rich food and pairs nicely with the tomato sauce, vegetables and noodles in this dish. The gluten-free noodles taste almost identical to their counterpart when cooked with all the lasagna fillings. Instead of meat, we are using chickpeas mashed with mushrooms! The beauty of vegan, gluten-free cooking is that when it's made right, it's delicious enough for everyone at the table to enjoy.

1 (14-oz [400-g]) can chickpeas, drained

1 cup (70 g) finely chopped cremini mushrooms

1 tbsp (15 ml) extra-virgin olive oil

1 tsp lemon juice

½ tsp sea salt

1 batch All-Purpose Tomato Sauce (page 101), divided

1 (10-oz [280-g]) box uncooked gluten-free lasagna noodles

5 cups (150 g) baby spinach, divided

½ batch Basil Arugula Pesto with Walnuts (page 97), divided

1–2 cups (112–224 g) shredded gluten-free vegan mozzarella or Parmesan, or as desired, divided

¼ cup (10 g) finely chopped fresh basil

Preheat the oven to 375°F (190°C).

In a large bowl, add the chickpeas and mash them with a potato masher or a fork until you have a chunky mixture. You don't need them to be a paste; you just want to break apart their structure so they stick to the lasagna. Add the mushrooms, olive oil, lemon juice and sea salt and mix it all up with a spoon. Set aside.

In a square or rectangular baking dish (whatever best fits your lasagna noodles), add ½ cup (120 ml) of the tomato sauce and your first layer of noodles. Add ½ cup (82 g) of the chickpea-mushroom mixture and a handful of spinach. Scoop on a few spoonfuls of the pesto, and sprinkle on some shredded vegan cheese. Repeat your layering until the pan is full! If needed, press it all down as you go. (The spinach takes up a lot of room but will cook down once it's in the oven.) Make sure your lasagna is topped with the wet ingredients and not the noodles. Cover the top of the lasagna with an oiled piece of tinfoil so it doesn't burn. Bake for 45 minutes, or until the noodles are soft and the juices bubbling up around the edges have reduced. Remove the tinfoil and bake for 10 to 15 minutes, or until the top begins to brown. Let it cool for 15 minutes, top with the basil and enjoy! This will keep for 1 week in the fridge.

Blended Snacks, Sides and Breakfasts

These recipes are a mix of savory and sweet, for light nutrient-packed bites to get the day started right (or keep it going). Some of these recipes are terrific pick-me-ups between meals, some can be added to your favorite mains as side dishes and some are intended more as breakfast recipes. But I firmly believe we can eat whatever we want at whatever time we want. So go ahead and make pancakes for dinner!

Zucchini Chickpea Fritters with Cashew Sauce

YIELD: 8 FRITTERS

These fritters look impressive and complex to make, but they actually come together in under 30 minutes without much work. They make a wonderful snack on their own, with a dip or sauce or added to entrees. I like them paired with my Creamy Dressing with Chipotle and Nutritional Yeast (page 105).

Look for chickpea flour in Indian grocery stores or in the international food section of your typical grocery store. If you can't find it, you can use your regular ol' gluten-free flour blend!

2 large zucchinis (617 g), roughly chopped

1 (14-oz [400-g]) can chickpeas, drained

½ tsp sea salt

½ tsp smoked paprika powder

½ tsp chili powder

¼ tsp coriander powder

⅓ cup (53 g) roughly chopped onion

2 cloves garlic (14 g), peeled and roughly chopped

½ cup (69 g) chickpea flour or gluten-free flour blend, or more as needed

Mild vegetable oil, as needed

⅓ cup (60 ml) Creamy Dressing with Chipotle and Nutritional Yeast (page 105)

Pinch of cracked black pepper

Add the zucchini to your Vitamix and blend on low until it has a grated texture. This should only take a few seconds. Remove from your blender and let the zucchini sit in a sieve for 10 minutes so the moisture can drain out of it. Then, squeeze any excess water out by hand or with a spoon.

Add the chickpeas, salt, paprika, chili, coriander, onion and garlic. Blend on low until the texture is crumbly and wet. Transfer to a large bowl and add the zucchini and flour. Mix with a spoon until you have a thick, chunky mixture that you can form into patties. Add more flour in ¼-cup (35-g) increments if it's still too wet. Form into patties, and cook in a generous amount of oil in a nonstick pan over medium or medium-high heat. You want your pan to be hot enough that when you add the patties, they begin to gently sizzle. Cook for 4 to 5 minutes on each side. They're done when they're brown and crispy! Serve drizzled with the creamy dressing and some black pepper. These will keep in the fridge for 1 week.

Cheesy Kale Chips with Hemp Seeds

YIELD: 5–6 SERVINGS (1 BIG BOWL)

This recipe will make eating your greens an effortless experience. Kale chips have become a trendy food and for good reason. Instead of eating a plate of raw greens with a dressing, we are essentially baking our salad into a crunchy, savory bowl of chips! Some recipes simply use oil and salt as the dressing, but I like to turn my kale chips up a notch and use a creamy, nutty, cheesy sauce to coat them. We add some hemp seeds for extra nutrition and texture.

FOR THE SAUCE

¼ cup (65 g) Cashew Butter (page 128)

¼ cup (60 ml) mild vegetable oil

⅓ cup (80 ml) water

3 tbsp (15 g) nutritional yeast flakes

3 tbsp (45 ml) gluten-free tamari

1 tbsp (15 ml) lemon juice

1 clove garlic (7 g), peeled and roughly chopped

½ tsp black pepper

½ tsp smoked paprika powder

½ tsp onion powder

FOR THE BASE

2 bunches (400 g) curly kale

¼ cup (40 g) hemp seeds

Preheat the oven to 300°F (150°C). Line two baking sheets with parchment paper.

To make the sauce, blend all of the sauce ingredients in your Vitamix, until smooth. Adjust according to taste.

To make the base, wash the kale, and then rip the leaves off the stems. Add the leaves to a large bowl and coat them in the sauce. Get in there with your hands and massage the sauce into the leaves. Sprinkle on the hemp seeds. Arrange evenly in one layer on your baking sheet, and bake for 20 to 25 minutes, or until the kale pieces are getting crunchy on the edges. If your oven doesn't heat very evenly, rearrange the pans halfway through baking. Let it cool for 10 minutes so the chips can crisp up even more, and then enjoy! These will keep for 5 days, but I am quite sure they'll be gone the day you make them.

Salted Chocolate Almond Butter Cups

YIELD: 5 SERVINGS

The peanut butter cup has been elevated! There is nothing wrong with peanut butter, but when you feel like doing something a little different (and decadent), try making these simple almond butter cups. They are the perfect pick-me-up any time of day when you want a rich, satisfying treat.

FOR THE CHOCOLATE

⅓ cup (80 ml) melted coconut oil

⅓ cup (80 ml) maple syrup

2 tbsp (30 ml) rice syrup

⅓ cup (32 g) cocoa powder

¼ tsp vanilla extract

FOR THE ALMOND BUTTER FILLING

½ cup (129 g) almond butter

2 tbsp (30 ml) melted coconut oil

1 tsp unrefined cane sugar

½ tsp flaked salt (I use Maldon salt), for garnishing

Line a cupcake tin with cupcake liners or just have cupcake liners ready on their own.

To make the chocolate, add all of the chocolate ingredients to your Vitamix and blend until smooth. Set aside in a bowl.

To make the almond butter filling, add all of the almond butter ingredients to your Vitamix and blend until smooth.

Pour half of the chocolate mixture into the bottoms of the cupcake liners. Place in the freezer for 10 minutes, or until the chocolate has hardened. Pour the almond butter into each cupcake liner, and then top with your remaining chocolate. Sprinkle with flaked salt. Place in the freezer or fridge until they've solidified. Enjoy right away! These will keep for a few weeks in the fridge, or a couple months in the freezer.

Pancakes with Flaxseeds and Rolled Oats

YIELD: 6–8 MEDIUM PANCAKES

This is a quick and easy plant-based, gluten-free pancake recipe. I have made this many times for friends, family and romantic partners, and it always impresses. Thanks to the Vitamix, we can grind our own flour, which makes the pancakes taste extra fresh.

1 cup (240 ml) almond milk, or more as needed

¼ cup (23 g) gluten-free rolled oats

¾ cup (111 g) gluten-free all-purpose flour blend

1 tbsp (10 g) ground flaxseeds mixed with 3 tbsp (45 ml) water

2 tbsp (22 g) coconut sugar

1 tbsp (14 g) baking powder

1 tsp gluten-free cornstarch

½ tsp vanilla extract

¼ tsp sea salt

1 tbsp (14 g) coconut oil

Vegan margarine or mild vegetable oil, for cooking

Add all of the ingredients, except the margarine, to your Vitamix and blend. If it needs help blending, add more almond milk in ¼-cup (60-ml) increments. Let the batter sit for 5 minutes while you heat the margarine in a nonstick pan over medium heat. Pour the batter into the pan, sizing your pancakes as you like. I recommend ¼ cup (60 ml). They should begin to sizzle once you pour the batter on, otherwise your pan is not hot enough. Turn the heat down to medium-low and cook for 5 to 6 minutes on each side, or until they begin to brown. Add margarine in 1-tablespoon (15-g) increments as needed.

Enjoy right away! Serve the pancakes with any and all toppings you like (suggestions: fruit, coconut whipped cream and chocolate chips). These will keep for 3 to 4 days in the fridge.

Blueberry Oat Pancakes with Coconut Butter Spread

YIELD: 4–6 MEDIUM PANCAKES

Classic for a reason, blueberry pancakes are the perfect decadent start to any day! These are full of fiber and nutrients, thanks to rolled oats and chia seeds, but taste as good as any traditional pancake recipe. We top the pancakes with rich and creamy coconut butter for a game-changing combo. Feel free to switch out the blueberries for any other fruit or treat and the coconut butter for nut butter. (For example: bananas and almond butter or chocolate chips and hazelnut butter.)

FOR THE BATTER

1 cup (240 ml) almond milk, or more as needed

¼ cup (23 g) gluten-free rolled oats

¾ cup (111 g) gluten-free all-purpose flour blend

1 tbsp (10 g) ground flaxseeds mixed with 3 tbsp (45 ml) water

2 tbsp (22 g) coconut sugar

1 tbsp (14 g) baking powder

1 tsp gluten-free cornstarch

½ tsp vanilla extract

¼ tsp sea salt

1 tbsp (14 g) coconut oil

½ tsp cinnamon powder

½ tsp ginger powder

1 cup (148 g) fresh or frozen blueberries

FOR COOKING AND SERVING

Vegan margarine or mild vegetable oil

Coconut Butter (page 132), for serving

Maple syrup, for serving

Fresh blueberries, for serving

Coconut shreds, for serving

Add all of the batter ingredients, except the blueberries, to your Vitamix and blend. If it needs help blending, add more almond milk in ¼-cup (60-ml) increments. Gently fold in the blueberries by hand. Make sure not to overmix (unless you want pink pancakes).

Let the batter sit for 5 minutes while you heat the margarine in a nonstick pan over medium heat. Pour the batter into the pan, sizing your pancakes as you like. I recommend ¼ cup (60 ml) of batter per pancake. They should begin to sizzle once you pour the batter on, otherwise your pan is not hot enough. Turn the heat down to medium-low and cook for 5 to 6 minutes on each side, or until they begin to brown. Add more margarine in 1-tablespoon (15-g) increments as needed. Enjoy right away! Serve the pancakes with Coconut Butter, maple syrup, more blueberries, coconut shreds and any and all toppings you like. These will keep for 3 to 4 days in the fridge, with toppings stored separately.

Wholesome Muffins with Pecans and Walnuts

YIELD: 12 MUFFINS

These muffins are hearty and wholesome, yet light and tender. With a hint of cinnamon, vanilla and sugar, they're the perfect snack or light breakfast with just the right amount of sweetness. In vegan baking, we use ground flaxseeds mixed with water as the binder, instead of eggs.

FOR THE MUFFINS

½ cup (100 g) unrefined cane sugar

¼ cup (57 g) margarine or ¼ cup (60 ml) mild vegetable oil

1 cup (240 ml) non-dairy milk

2 tbsp (20 g) ground flaxseeds mixed with ¼ cup (60 ml) water

1 tsp vanilla extract

1½ cups (125 g) all-purpose gluten-free flour blend

½ cup (45 g) gluten-free rolled oats

1 tbsp (8 g) gluten-free cornstarch*

1 tsp baking soda

1 tsp baking powder

½ tsp sea salt

½ tsp cinnamon powder

FOR THE TOPPINGS

½ cup (55 g) raw pecan pieces

½ cup (59 g) raw walnut pieces

½ cup (55 g) brown sugar

½ tsp cinnamon powder

1 tsp vanilla extract

2 tbsp (30 ml) melted non-dairy margarine

Preheat the oven to 350°F (180°C). Line a large muffin pan with muffin liners.

To make the muffins, add the sugar and margarine to your Vitamix and blend until evenly combined. Add the milk, flax mixture and vanilla and blend until smooth. Add the flour, oats, cornstarch, baking soda, baking powder, salt and cinnamon and blend until evenly combined. Scoop your muffin mixture evenly into the liners, filling each one no more than two-thirds full.

To make the topping, in a medium bowl, mix together all the ingredients by hand. Add on top of the batter in the liners.

Bake the muffins for 25 to 30 minutes, or until a toothpick stuck in the middle of one comes out clean. Let cool and enjoy! These will keep at room temperature for 3 days, or in the fridge for 5 to 7 days.

* You can use arrowroot powder or tapioca powder instead of cornstarch.

Vegan Charcuterie Board

YIELD: SERVES A PARTY OF 8–12 PEOPLE

Sooo . . . I will be the first to admit this is not a traditional charcuterie board. At all. They usually revolve around cured meats and dairy cheeses. We are doing our own thing and using only plant-based and gluten-free foods, but that doesn't make it any less delicious! This is an impressive and crowd-pleasing party dish for any time of the year.

1 cup (225 g) pitted Medjool dates

½ cup (125 g) dried figs

1 pear (178 g), sliced and deseeded

1 green apple (182 g), sliced and deseeded

1 cup (150 g) grapes

½ cup (120 g) artichoke hearts, preserved in brine

½ cup (90 g) Castelvetrano olives, preserved in brine, pitted

½ cup (90 g) Kalamata olives, preserved in brine, pitted

½ cup (120 g) sun-dried tomatoes in olive oil

½ cup (54 g) toasted, blanched almonds

½ cup (75 g) grape tomatoes

1 batch Basil Arugula Pesto with Walnuts (page 97)

1 batch Pine Nut and Almond Herbed Cheese (page 114)

½ batch Hummus with Smoked Paprika (page 102)

Variety of gluten-free crackers or 1 batch Hemp Seed and Almond Rosemary Crackers (page 144)

6–8 sprigs of mint, basil and rosemary, for garnishing

Get out a big ol' wooden cutting board or marble pastry board. Or lay out parchment paper, linen towels or multiple plates on your table. Take a deep breath, get in touch with your inner artist and begin. Look up photos of charcuterie boards for inspiration, if you like.

Carefully and thoughtfully arrange all the different components on your board. Some ingredients like the dips, spreads and brine-cured foods will need to be served in little bowls. Others can be placed directly on your board or table, like the crackers and dried fruits.

Leave out small spoons and knives for your guests to scoop and spread the ingredients. Decorate with mint, basil and rosemary and enjoy!

Maple Nut Granola

YIELD: 4 CUPS (410 G)

The breakfast (or snack) of champions: granola. This sweet, rich recipe is full of healthy fats, fiber, B vitamins and vitamins and minerals including zinc, calcium, iron and copper. We sweeten oats and nuts with maple syrup and brown sugar for a caramel-like flavor. This is lovely paired with coconut yogurt, on ice cream, in place of cereal or on its own outta the jar!

2 cups (180 g) gluten-free rolled oats

1 cup (146 g) raw cashews

1 cup (109 g) raw pecans

⅓ cup (80 ml) maple syrup

⅓ cup (73 g) brown sugar

¼ cup (60 ml) melted refined coconut oil

1 tsp vanilla extract

½ tsp sea salt

Preheat the oven to 350°F (180°C). Line a baking sheet with parchment paper.

Scoop ¼ cup each of your oats, cashews and pecans into your Vitamix. Blend until you have a fine flour-y texture. Put in a bowl and set aside. Blend the maple syrup, brown sugar, coconut oil, vanilla and sea salt, until smooth. In a large bowl, evenly coat your remaining unblended oats, cashews and pecans with the maple syrup mixture. Add the blended flour-y mixture and mix until everything is evenly coated. Spread your coated oats and nuts out onto the baking sheet.

Bake for 30 minutes, or until the granola is golden brown and fragrant. Mix the granola around after 15 minutes so it bakes evenly. This will keep for 2 weeks at room temperature or in the fridge.

Luscious Sweet Treats

If you're familiar with my first cookbook, *Rawsome Vegan Baking*, you know I am a devout lover of all things sweet. Sugar and I are just buds, what can I say? When I went vegan over a decade ago, I quickly realized I didn't have to give up delicious desserts while keeping a fairly whole-foods diet. I personally think there's a place for all kinds of sweet treats, and we never need to feel guilt for anything we eat. I love wholesome treats as much as I enjoy treats that have more refined ingredients. They all make me happy, so they're all good for me. That being said, this cookbook is keeping things wholesome and nutrient-dense, so these desserts generously offer a lot of hidden nutrition and whole-foods goodness. These are nearly all quick to make and perfect to share with a friend or lover.

Simple Chocolate Fudge

YIELD: 1 CUP (240 ML)

This is a super quick and easy recipe that you'll be making the rest of your life! Er, I mean I don't want to assume . . . but I feel pretty confident. Thanks to the thick consistency of the rice syrup, this works as a thick sauce when it's left at room temperature and turns into fudge when it's refrigerated. If you'd like a thinner consistency for plain ol' chocolate sauce, use liquid coconut oil and/or replace the rice syrup with more maple syrup.

⅓ cup (32 g) cocoa powder

⅓ cup (80 ml) melted coconut oil

¼ cup (60 ml) maple syrup

⅓ cup (80 ml) rice syrup

¼ tsp vanilla extract (optional)

⅛ tsp sea salt (optional)

Add all of the ingredients to your Vitamix and blend for 10 to 20 seconds, or until smooth. It's that simple! Use right away on ice cream, fruit or whatever you desire. This will keep in the fridge for 1 month.

Chocolate Date Milkshake

YIELD: 3½ CUPS (840 ML)

This is my absolute favorite nutrient-packed milkshake. There's nothing wrong with indulging in a milkshake with actual ice cream (I would still keep it plant-based, but that's just me). But when I feel like getting some good stuff in me without drinking something particularly fruity or green-tasting, or a super-sweet and rich, traditional milkshake, I make this. It's creamy, chocolatey, sweet but not too sweet, and slightly nutty thanks to the oat milk and cashew butter.

2 frozen bananas (236 g), chopped into 1" (2.5-cm) pieces

2 Medjool dates, pitted

2 tbsp (11 g) cacao powder

3 tbsp (45 ml) maple syrup

2 tbsp (32 g) Cashew Butter (page 128)

½ tsp vanilla extract

1 tsp adaptogenic mushroom powder (I like Lion's Mane; optional)

1 cup (240 ml) Oat Milk (page 139) or other non-dairy milk, plus more if needed

2–3 ice cubes (optional)

¼ cup (60 ml) Simple Chocolate Fudge (page 74)

Add all of the ingredients, except the chocolate fudge, to your Vitamix and blend for 30 seconds, or until smooth. Add more milk and/or ice cubes, if desired. Pour into one or two glasses and garnish with the chocolate fudge. Enjoy right away!

Coconut Milkshake with Salted Caramel

YIELD: 2 CUPS (480 ML)

I looooove vanilla milkshakes. When I went vegan ten years ago, I thought it meant giving up this ice cream treat. I was wrong! We can make delicious vegan milkshakes using rich coconut milk and frozen bananas. In this recipe, we are adding a sweet-and-salty caramel for an extra layer of goodness.

P.S. If you want an even more indulgent experience, you can use vegan ice cream instead of bananas.

1 (13.5-oz [398-ml]) can full-fat coconut milk, left in the fridge overnight

3 frozen bananas (354 g), chopped into 1" (2.5-cm) pieces

½ tsp vanilla extract

1 tbsp (15 ml) maple syrup

½ cup (129 g) Caramel Cashew Butter (page 131) or Salted Date Caramel (page 90)

¼ cup (60 ml) non-dairy milk

Scoop out the thicker, almost solid coconut milk in the can. Keep this thick stuff, and set aside the thinner white liquid that remains. Add the thick coconut milk to your Vitamix, along with the bananas, vanilla and maple syrup. Blend until the mixture becomes thick and smooth, like soft-serve ice cream. If it's too thick, add some of the thinner white liquid from the can of coconut milk you set aside. Stop blending as soon as it's smooth. Pour into glasses.

Add the caramel and milk to your Vitamix and blend for a few seconds. You simply want the caramel to be a little thinner for this recipe. Scoop the caramel onto your milkshakes, and stir it in a little so it's evenly swirled inside the glass. Enjoy right away!

Raspberry Sorbetto

YIELD: 3 CUPS (720 ML)

Sorbet is my favorite summer treat, and with a Vitamix I can make it right at home!
Not only is this way more affordable, but it also allows me to customize the flavors according
to what I'm craving. Mango and banana make the whole recipe super creamy; pineapple adds
a little tartness to balance the sweetness; and raspberry gives that beautiful color
and mouthwatering flavor.

¾ cup (124 g) frozen mango chunks

¾ cup (124 g) frozen pineapple chunks

¾ cup (92 g) frozen raspberries, plus more for garnishing

1 banana (118 g), peeled and broken up into chunks

1 tsp lime juice

Pinch of stevia powder (optional)

Add all of the ingredients to your Vitamix and blend for 30 to 60 seconds, or until smooth and raspberry pink. Use the tamper to keep pushing the frozen mixture down towards the blades. Stop blending as soon as the mixture is smooth, otherwise you risk over-blending and melting the sorbetto. Garnish with more raspberries if you like! Scoop into bowls and enjoy right away!

Chocolate Avocado Frosting

YIELD: APPROXIMATELY 3 CUPS (720 G)

This can be enjoyed as a frosting for cakes, a pudding on its own or even as a dip for fruits! The idea of avocado going into a sweet chocolate recipe may be off-putting to many, but try it anyway! The avocado flavor is subtle and mostly masked by the cocoa and syrups, so we get to benefit from its rich creaminess and slight nutty flavor. The only disadvantage to this recipe is that it's best fresh and eaten within a few days. So plan to make it for special occasions with guests, or cut the recipe in half for a smaller amount if you're not using it on a cake.

3 medium avocados (450 g), pitted

½ cup (44 g) cocoa powder

½ cup (120 ml) brown rice syrup

3 tbsp (45 ml) maple syrup

⅓ cup (80 ml) melted coconut oil

1 tsp vanilla extract

¼ tsp sea salt

¼ cup (60 ml) non-dairy milk, or more if preferred (optional)

Add all of the ingredients to your Vitamix and blend until thick and smooth. If you're using it for pudding or dip, or you just want it thinner, add non-dairy milk in ¼-cup (60-ml) increments. If you're using it for cake, keep it thick and leave as is. Frost your cake immediately, or scoop into a sealable container and leave in the fridge until you're ready to use it.

Chocolate Blender Cake

The advantage of making gluten-free baked goods in a Vitamix is that we don't have to stress as much about over-blending. Over-blending, which can easily happen in a blender, typically causes the development of too much gluten protein. This results in chewy, gummy baked goods. We aren't using gluten, so we don't have to worry about that.

The best gluten-free flour is a blend of multiple different kinds. I like Bob's Red Mill, King Arthur or GoGo Quinoa gluten-free flour blends. Since we have no gluten to help bind the recipe, we are using two different binders: cornstarch *and* flaxseeds. This helps keep our cake from being crumbly.

This cake is moist, lightly sweet, nutty and somehow still manages to be nutritious *and* decadent at the same time.

Psst: This recipe works for cupcakes, too!

1½ cups (188 g) all-purpose gluten-free flour blend

½ cup (56 g) almond flour

1 cup (200 g) unrefined cane sugar

½ cup (44 g) cocoa powder

½ tsp sea salt

½ tsp gluten-free cornstarch

1 tsp baking soda

1 tsp baking powder

1 tbsp (7 g) ground flaxseeds mixed with 3 tbsp (45 ml) water

1 tsp vanilla extract

1 cup (225 g) non-dairy margarine or (240 ml) vegetable oil

1 cup (240 ml) non-dairy milk, plus more if needed

Preheat the oven to 350°F (180°C). Line two 6-inch (15-cm) (for thicker cakes) or 9-inch (23-cm) (for thinner cakes) cake pans with parchment paper, margarine or oil. Or line a cupcake pan with cupcake liners.

Add the flour, almond flour, sugar, cocoa powder, salt, cornstarch, baking soda and baking powder to your Vitamix and blend for 5 seconds, or until all the ingredients are evenly combined. Add the flaxseed mixture, vanilla, margarine and milk and blend until everything is evenly combined. If it's too thick, add 1 more cup (240 ml) of milk in ¼-cup (60-ml) increments. Stop as soon as it's blended!

Pour the batter evenly into the cake or cupcake pan(s). Bake for 30 to 40 minutes, or until the tops are bouncy and a fork inserted in the center of the cakes comes out clean. Let them cool completely before frosting.

Chocolate Cake with Avocado Frosting

YIELD: 1 TWO-TIER CAKE OR 8-12 SERVINGS

This is a beautiful, elegant, mouthwatering cake for all to enjoy! As with all the recipes in this book, this is vegan, gluten-free and magically full of nutritious ingredients.

P.S. I know not everyone is gonna love avocado in their frosting. It's not for every palate! So feel free to use your own favorite plant-based frosting in this recipe.

1 batch Chocolate Blender Cake (page 85)

1 batch Chocolate Avocado Frosting (page 82) or your favorite vegan frosting

¼ cup (42 g) dark chocolate, finely chopped or shaved

Pinch of flaked salt (optional)

Frost the top of your first cake evenly, and then add the second cake on top. Frost the top of the second cake evenly. It's a matter of preference to frost the sides of the cake or leave them naked, so I will let you decide. Once your cake is frosted, sprinkle the chocolate and salt, if using, on top. Feel free to add fresh or dried fruits, like raspberries, for some color! Slice and enjoy right away! This will keep in the fridge for 3 to 4 days.

Baked Pears with Spiced Almond Butter

YIELD: 4 BAKED PEARS

This is an elegant dessert that is sure to impress any guest or loved one! These baked pears look and taste fancy, but they're actually really easy and quick to prepare. The aromatics of cinnamon, vanilla, maple syrup and toasted almonds all work perfectly together to add some depth to the sweet, juicy softness of the pears.

P.S. If you can get your hands on some real vanilla bean to add to the pears, it's so worth it.

FOR THE BAKED PEARS
4 Anjou pears (712 g), halved and cored

¼ cup (60 ml) maple syrup

1 tbsp (15 ml) melted coconut oil

½ tsp cinnamon powder

½ tsp vanilla extract

¼ tsp vanilla bean seeds (optional)

FOR THE SPICED ALMOND BUTTER DRIZZLE
¼ cup (65 g) Spiced Almond Butter with Cinnamon and Maca (page 127)

1–3 tbsp (15–45 ml) non-dairy milk, as needed

ADDITIONAL PAIRING IDEAS
Non-dairy ice cream

Cultured Coconut Yogurt (page 143)

Preheat the oven to 375°F (190°C). Line a baking sheet with parchment paper.

To make the pears, arrange the pear halves, cored flesh sides facing up, on the baking sheet. In a large bowl, mix together the rest of the pear ingredients either by hand or in your Vitamix. Drizzle this mixture over the pears and bake for 20 to 25 minutes, or until they are softened and beginning to brown.

To make the drizzle, in a bowl, mix together the almond butter and non-dairy milk in 1-tablespoon (15-ml) increments until it's a consistency you can drizzle over your pears. Drizzle the almond butter mixture over your baked pears and enjoy right away! I recommend serving with plant-based vanilla ice cream. This recipe will keep for 2 to 3 days in the fridge.

Salted Date Caramel

YIELD: 1½ CUPS (360 ML)

Medjool dates are a staple in almost any vegan kitchen, and here we put them to work in a luxurious salted caramel recipe. I love to use this as a dip for apples, a spread for brownies, a drizzle on ice cream . . . It's also fabulous eaten on its own with a spoon. You can make (or buy) more traditional-style caramel using coconut milk and sugar, and it's delicious! But I like to use this recipe more often since I can make it quickly and easily in my blender, and it's more nutrient-dense because the base is dates (i.e. dried fruit!).

1 cup (225 g) pitted Medjool dates

⅓ cup (80 ml) melted coconut oil

¼ cup (60 ml) non-dairy milk, plus more if needed

½ tsp vanilla extract

1 tbsp (15 ml) maple syrup or coconut nectar (optional)

¼ tsp sea salt

Add all of the ingredients to your Vitamix and blend for 10 seconds. Add more milk in 1-tablespoon (15-ml) increments until you achieve the consistency you desire. Use immediately or store in the fridge for 3 to 4 days.

Easy Sauces, Dips and Spreads

Oh, baby! This is one of my favorite chapters because it provides the essentials for most of the Vitamixed Mains (page 35). In other words, these recipes hold all the keys to the realm of flavor. And par for the course, they're quick and easy to make. For the most part, we are just going to throw a bunch of stuff in our Vitamix and then blend, blend, blend. These recipes are perfect bases for any delicious plant-based meal, and I recommend keeping them in your fridge at all times! Then, when you want a yummy lunch or dinner but don't feel like putting in too much effort, you can simply cook some rice, steam some vegetables and add one of these sauces on top. Bam. Done. Voilà! Making these kinds of recipes at home in the blender not only saves you money, it's also a reminder of how capable you are. Heck *yes* you can make your own pesto. And it tastes *better* than the stuff from the store! As an added bonus, making your own sauces and marinades tends to impress friends, guests . . . and potential love interests.

Navy Bean Dip with Roasted Bell Pepper

YIELD: 3 CUPS (720 G)

If you like hummus, you will LOVE this! It's a smoky, creamy dip made from white beans and roasted red pepper. Plant-based dips and spreads are absolutely divine when they're made fresh in your blender. Store-bought varieties, even the fancy ones, just don't compare.

2 fresh red bell peppers (300 g), sliced in half lengthwise and deseeded

⅓ cup (80 ml) extra-virgin olive oil, plus 2 tbsp (30 ml) for cooking

4 cloves garlic (28 g), peeled and minced

¼ cup (40 g) white onion, peeled and minced

½–1 tsp sea salt

½ tsp coriander powder

¼ tsp cracked black pepper

¼ tsp smoked paprika powder

1 (14-oz [400-g]) can navy beans, rinsed and drained

¼ cup (60 ml) water, or more as needed

¼ cup (60 ml) lemon juice

Preheat the oven to 475°F (240°C). Line a baking sheet with parchment paper.

Arrange the bell pepper halves on the baking sheet with the insides facing down. Roast for 30 to 40 minutes, or until the peppers are slightly charred and wrinkled. Remove from the oven and let cool.

While your bell peppers are roasting, prepare the other ingredients. In a large nonstick pan over medium heat, heat 2 tablespoons (30 ml) of the olive oil. Add the garlic, onion, salt, coriander, pepper and paprika, and cook for 5 minutes. Add the navy beans and cook for 5 minutes. Remove from the heat and let cool for 15 to 20 minutes.

Add the roasted bell peppers and the sautéed bean mixture to your Vitamix. Add the remaining olive oil along with the water and lemon juice, and blend for 30 to 60 seconds. If you want it to be thinner, add water in ¼-cup (60-ml) increments. Adjust according to taste, adding more salt or spices, as desired. Enjoy with chips, crackers, vegetables, pasta . . . anything, really! I recommend garnishing with extra olive oil, flaked salt, paprika powder and some finely chopped basil or parsley. This will keep in the fridge for 7 days.

Basil Arugula Pesto with Walnuts

YIELD: 2 CUPS (480 ML)

Pesto is the best-o: It's rich, creamy, bursting with flavor and tastes great on just about everything savory. Traditional pesto uses basil, pine nuts and parmesan. We are going in a different direction here, and using a variety of herbs and nuts, including arugula and walnuts.

2 cups (48 g) packed basil leaves

1 cup (50 g) packed arugula leaves

1 cup (117 g) raw walnuts

½ cup (68 g) raw pine nuts

½ cup (120 ml) extra-virgin olive oil, plus more if needed

2 cloves garlic (14 g), peeled and minced, plus more to taste

1 tbsp (15 ml) lemon juice, plus more if needed

½ tsp sea salt, plus more to taste

Add all of the ingredients to your Vitamix and blend in short bursts for 1 minute, or until everything is well combined. Add more lemon juice and olive oil as needed to help the mixture blend. Continue blending until you have a creamy pesto. Adjust according to taste, adding more lemon juice, olive oil, salt or garlic, as desired.

Buttery Spread with Herbs and Garlic

YIELD: ¾ CUP AND 1 TABLESPOON (200 ML)

This is my absolute favorite herbed vegan buttery recipe. This isn't a replacement for butter in baking, but it's fabulous on pasta, sandwiches and roasted vegetables. It's full of healthy fats and bursting with flavor from the garlic and herbs. Hemp seeds add protein and a lil fiber, too!

¼ cup (60 ml) melted coconut oil

⅓ cup (80 ml) extra-virgin olive oil

¼ cup (40 g) hemp seeds

1 tsp garlic powder or flakes, plus more to taste

1 tsp nutritional yeast flakes

½ tsp sea salt, plus more to taste

¼ tsp dried rosemary leaves, finely chopped (optional)

¼ tsp dried thyme leaves, finely chopped (optional)

Add all of the ingredients, except the herbs, to your Vitamix and blend for 30 seconds, or until smooth. Adjust according to taste and blend once more, adding more salt or garlic, if desired. Stir in the rosemary and thyme by hand. Pour into a jar and leave at room temperature. It will thicken once it cools down. This will keep in the fridge for 2 months.

All-Purpose Tomato Sauce

YIELD: 4 CUPS (960 ML)

This is a simple, from-scratch tomato sauce recipe for all your tomato needs! You can use it on pasta, in other sauces, in curries and beyond. I like roasting my tomatoes before blending them because it imparts a rich, smoky flavor that balances well with the natural acidity of tomatoes.

4 lb (1.8 kg) fresh, ripe tomatoes

5 cloves garlic (35 g), peeled

3 tbsp (45 ml) extra-virgin olive oil

2 tsp (10 ml) lemon juice

1 tsp sea salt

½ tsp unrefined cane sugar

Preheat the oven to 400°F (200°C). Line a baking sheet with parchment paper.

Core the stems from the tomatoes, and slice the tomatoes in half. Arrange the tomato halves on the baking sheet with the insides facing down. Sprinkle the garlic among the tomato halves. Roast for 30 to 40 minutes, or until the tomatoes begin to brown and get juicy and wrinkly. Keep an eye on the garlic, making sure it doesn't burn. Remove from the oven and let cool. If desired, remove the tomato skins.

Add the cooled tomatoes and garlic to your Vitamix. Blend for 1 minute, or until as smooth as you would like. Add the oil, lemon juice, salt and sugar and pulse until fully incorporated. If you'd like your sauce thicker, reduce the sauce in a large nonstick pan over medium-low heat until it reaches the consistency you prefer. Store in freezer-safe containers or resealable bags. This will keep in the freezer for up to 6 months or in the fridge for 1 month.

Notes: I highly recommend finding some local, organic tomatoes to make this with. When you start with the freshest produce, you will end up with the most delicious product.

Some people like to remove the tomato skins, but I prefer to keep them on. If you want to remove them, do so after they've been roasted and have cooled down.

Hummus with Smoked Paprika

YIELD: 3 CUPS (720 G)

Ahh, hummus. It's a vegan mainstay that's cheap and quick to make, and the best part is obviously that it's delicious. Hummus is essentially a creamy chickpea and tahini dip, flavored with garlic, lemon and spices. Its origins are in the Middle East (beginning way back in the thirteenth century), where it's often eaten with pita bread.

1 (14-oz [400-g]) can chickpeas, rinsed and drained

½ cup (120 ml) extra-virgin olive oil, plus 1 tbsp (15 ml) for garnishing

⅓ cup (80 ml) tahini

¼ cup (60 ml) lemon juice

1 tsp sea salt

½ tsp garlic powder

2 cloves garlic (14 g), peeled and minced

½ cup (120 ml) water, or more as needed

½ tsp flaked salt (I use Maldon salt), for garnishing

¼ tsp smoked paprika powder, for garnishing

Add all of the ingredients to your Vitamix, except the water and garnishings. Blend for 1 minute, and then add the water in ¼-cup (60-ml) increments until you have the consistency you prefer. (I like mine thick.) The longer you blend, the smoother it will be. Give your blender short breaks to cool down, if needed. Garnish with a drizzle of olive oil, the flaked salt and smoked paprika. Enjoy right away with anything savory! This will keep for 1 week in the fridge.

Creamy Dressing with Chipotle and Nutritional Yeast

YIELD: 2 CUPS (480 ML)

Oh, baby, this is GOOD. My favorite salad dressings to buy are Yeshi and Little Creek (both local to my home province of British Columbia, Canada). Yeshi is a thick, creamy, nutritional yeast–based dressing. Little Creek is a thinner, tangy dressing with lots of tamari and lemon. This recipe is a marriage between the two . . . and excellent on everything, not just salad.

⅓ cup (24 g) nutritional yeast flakes

¼ cup (36 g) raw cashews, soaked for 30 minutes in water, and then rinsed and drained

½ tsp chipotle powder

½ tsp garlic powder

¼ tsp sea salt

½ cup (120 ml) water, or more as needed

2 tbsp (30 ml) lemon juice

¼ cup (60 ml) gluten-free tamari

½ cup (120 ml) mild vegetable oil (like sunflower, canola or avocado)

1 clove garlic (7 g), peeled and roughly chopped

1 tsp maple syrup

Add all of the ingredients to your Vitamix and blend for 30 seconds, or until totally smooth. If it's too thick, add more water in 1-tablespoon (15-ml) increments. Adjust according to taste, adding more of anything you like! This will keep in the fridge for 2 to 3 weeks.

Note: The dressing will thicken up when it stays in the fridge. This is normal. Just add some extra water or lemon juice, or keep it thick!

BBQ Sauce with Tamarind and Orange

YIELD: 4 CUPS (960 ML)

Even though it was originally created to complement foods on the grill, barbeque sauce is heavenly on nearly every savory dish. It's sweet, smoky, tangy and salty all at once. I love tomatoes, and since they are the base of BBQ sauce, it's no surprise I keep this in my fridge at all times. My take on BBQ sauce includes tamarind paste and just a hint of orange. Tamarind paste comes from a sweet, tart fruit and is often used in Thai, Vietnamese, Latin and Caribbean cooking. Tamarind is also a key ingredient in Worcestershire sauce, which is a staple in BBQ sauce! So here we are swapping out the Worcestershire (which is usually not vegan) for pure tamarind paste.

2 cups (480 ml) tomato sauce

¼ cup (60 ml) tomato paste

⅓ cup (80 ml) apple cider vinegar

¼ cup (60 ml) maple syrup

¼ cup (60 ml) tamarind paste concentrate or a tamarind-based sauce*

⅓ cup (73 g) brown sugar

3 tbsp (45 ml) molasses

1 tbsp (15 ml) orange juice

½ tsp orange zest

1 clove garlic (7 g), peeled and roughly chopped

1 tsp garlic powder

¾ tsp smoked paprika powder

½ tsp onion powder

½ tsp cracked black pepper

¼ tsp liquid smoke

2 tsp (12 g) sea salt

Add all of the ingredients to your Vitamix, and blend for 30 to 60 seconds, or until completely smooth. Adjust according to taste preferences. Feel free to add more spices, salt or sweetener. This will keep in the fridge for 1 month.

Tamarind paste or concentrate can usually be found in Indian or Asian grocery stores. If you have no luck there, look online! You want an actual paste, not the hard brick of tamarind that is sometimes called tamarind paste. If you cannot find tamarind paste, you can use a store-bought sauce that includes tamarind.

Ginger Tahini Tofu Marinade

YIELD: ⅔ CUP (160 ML)

This marinade takes tofu (or anything you feel like marinating) from "okay" to "GIVE ME MORE!" Peanut oil adds a nice nuttiness that balances out all the other tangy, sweet and salty ingredients. Bonus: This recipe also makes a fantastic salad dressing.

2 tbsp (30 ml) peanut oil* or sesame oil

3 tbsp (48 g) tahini

¼ cup (60 ml) gluten-free tamari

1 tbsp (5 g) peeled and roughly chopped fresh ginger

3 cloves garlic (21 g), peeled and roughly chopped

1 tbsp (15 ml) rice vinegar, plus more if needed

3 tbsp (30 g) unrefined cane sugar

1 tbsp (14 g) brown sugar

½ tsp chili powder, or as desired

If you don't have peanut oil in your kitchen, you can use any other mild-tasting oil.

Add all of the ingredients to your Vitamix and blend until smooth. Adjust according to taste. You are now ready to marinate tofu . . . or anything else! This will keep on its own in the fridge for 5 days.

Cashew Queso

YIELD: 2 CUPS (480 ML)

Cue glorious music. This cheesy spread is absolutely fantastic on basically anything savory. The base is cashews, and then we add big flavor with liquid smoke, spices, lemon juice and a hint of mustard. I need this in my fridge at all times.

2 cups (292 g) raw cashews

¼ cup (20 g) nutritional yeast flakes

½ tsp liquid smoke

½ tsp smoked paprika powder

¼ tsp chili powder

½ tsp garlic powder

¼ tsp turmeric powder

1 tsp yellow mustard

2 tbsp (30 ml) extra-virgin olive oil

2 tbsp (30 ml) lemon juice

1 tsp sea salt

¾ cup (180 ml) water, or more as needed

Add all of the ingredients to your Vitamix and blend until very smooth. Taste and adjust accordingly, adding more salt or spices as desired. Transfer to a jar and let cool before screwing the lid on. This will thicken up as it sets. Add more water if you want a thinner queso. It will keep in the fridge for 1 month.

Cheesy Sauce

YIELD: 4 CUPS (960 ML)

Eating dairy-free doesn't mean we have to live without comfort foods like cheese!
Looking at the ingredients of this recipe, you might be thinking, "Carrots, potatoes? Sounds
weird . . . this is *not* gonna make a good cheese sauce." That's fair. But just try it! I think this
sauce might just rock your world. It's super creamy, flavorful and a total game changer
if you love rich, savory sauces. That's the magic of Vitamix!

2½ cups (375 g) peeled and chopped potatoes, 1" (2.5-cm) pieces

⅔ cup (84 g) chopped carrots, 1" (2.5-cm) pieces

¼ cup (40 g) chopped onion, 1" (2.5-cm) pieces

2 cloves garlic (14 g), peeled

¾ cup (109 g) raw cashews

¼ cup (60 ml) mild vegetable oil (canola, sunflower, etc.)

2 tbsp (30 g) miso paste

2 tbsp (10 g) nutritional yeast flakes

1 tsp sea salt

¼ tsp chipotle powder

¼ tsp smoked paprika powder

¼ tsp turmeric powder

¼ tsp cracked black pepper

Bring a medium pot of water to boil. Add the potatoes and carrots and boil for 6 minutes. Add the onion and garlic and boil for 2 to 4 minutes, or until the potatoes and carrots are tender. Scoop out all the boiled veggies with a slotted spoon—don't dump the water though!—and add them to your Vitamix along with the remaining ingredients and 1 cup (240 ml) of the boiled veggie water.

Blend for 60 to 90 seconds, or until you get a creamy cheesy sauce. If it's too thick, add more of the boiled veggie water in ¼-cup (60-ml) increments. Adjust according to taste, adding more salt or spices if you like. Use right away or let cool before storing. It will keep in the fridge for 1 week.

Pine Nut and Almond Herbed Cheese

YIELD: 3 CUPS (700 G)

Pine nuts are ultra-creamy, and thus make a wonderful base for rich, plant-based cheeses. This is a thick, flavorful cheese that is excellent for vegan charcuterie boards!

1 cup (135 g) raw pine nuts

1 cup (143 g) blanched almonds

¼ cup (60 ml) lemon juice

1 tbsp (15 ml) sauerkraut or pickle brine

Contents of 2 vegan, gluten-free probiotic capsules

3 tbsp (16 g) herbes de Provence, divided

1 tsp smoked salt, divided

Add all of the ingredients, except the herbes de Provence and ½ teaspoon of the salt, to your Vitamix and blend until smooth. Sprinkle in 1 tablespoon (5 g) of the herbes de Provence by hand.

Roll up the cheese in a piece of parchment paper, and sprinkle on the remaining salt and herbs. Wrap the roll of cheese in parchment paper, plastic wrap or a cheesecloth. Let this sit at room temperature or in the fridge for 2 to 3 days, and then enjoy! You *can* eat it right away, but the flavor enhances with time. This will keep in the fridge for 3 weeks.

Olive Tapenade with Sun-Dried Tomatoes

YIELD: 2 CUPS (480 G)

My girlfriend works at a cafe in downtown Nanaimo, BC, called The Vault. It's a rad little spot with tons of delicious vegan-friendly fare. One of the most mouthwatering items you can find there is a tapenade (olive-based spread) made with roasted red pepper and sun-dried tomatoes. They put it on sandwiches, wraps and paninis. Tragically it's not for sale, so I figured out my own recipe. This tapenade is ultra-creamy—almost whipped—and rich with olive flavor. The sun-dried tomatoes and roasted peppers add zest and smoke. This is excellent on crackers, pasta, roasted vegetables or even on its own if you're an olive fanatic like me!

1 cup (180 g) pitted Castelvetrano olives, preserved in brine

½ cup (90 g) pitted Kalamata olives, preserved in brine

½ cup (27 g) sun-dried tomatoes, preserved in olive oil

⅓ cup (18 g) roasted red bell pepper, preserved in brine

1 tbsp (8 g) capers, preserved in brine

1 tbsp (8 g) minced garlic, plus more to taste

1 tbsp (15 ml) olive oil, plus more if needed

¼ tsp sea salt (optional)

½ tsp lemon juice (optional)

Drain the olives, tomatoes and bell pepper and add to your Vitamix. Blend for 5 seconds, or until you have a rough paste. Add the drained capers, garlic and olive oil. Blend until you have a smooth paste, adding more olive oil in 1-tablespoon (15-ml) increments if needed. Adjust according to taste, adding more garlic, if desired. You could also add a pinch of salt or a splash of lemon juice—it's totally up to you! This will keep for 1 month in the fridge.

Basic Blends

Ah, the humble "basics" chapter . . . humble *and* essential. Like the previous chapter, these recipes are the base for a lot of other recipes in this book. And beyond that, they're just great to have on hand in your kitchen for infinite reasons. For example, I love coming home from a busy afternoon, craving something rich and chocolaty, and then finding Chocolate Hazelnut Butter (page 123) in the fridge. I eat a couple spoonfuls, and then it's on with the day. How wonderful that I made that recipe a week ago so I can enjoy it now. Or being able to whip up my matcha latte in the morning with fresh, homemade Almond Milk (page 135). Once again, it's a moment I can feel gratitude (and let's be honest, save some money, too).

Hazelnut Butter

I adore the flavor of hazelnuts; there is just nothing else like it. So it makes sense that I would love hazelnut butter. But the first few times I tried making my own, it never turned out as creamy as the store-bought stuff. And when I would splurge on the store-bought stuff, it was delicious, but not super fresh-tasting. After doing my own Internet research, I learned that the trick to the richest, creamiest hazelnut butter involves: A) toasting your own nuts and B) being patient when blending—magic takes time.

4 cups (460 g) raw hazelnuts

½ tsp sea salt (optional)

Preheat the oven to 350°F (180°C). Line a baking sheet with parchment paper.

Evenly spread the raw hazelnuts on the baking sheet, and bake for 15 to 20 minutes, or until the hazelnuts begin to smell fragrant and appear golden brown. Be cautious and attentive here, because the nuts can quickly burn! Let the hazelnuts cool, and then remove the skins as much as possible by rubbing the nuts around in your hands or between a cloth. Removing the skins makes a creamier butter.

Add the hazelnuts to your Vitamix, and blend in 5-minute increments for 10 to 15 minutes, stopping whenever you need to scrape down the sides and give your blender a break so it doesn't overheat. It will take some time, but eventually the hazelnuts will transform into a wonderfully creamy butter. The longer you blend, the creamier it gets as the oils are released. Add the salt, if using, just before you're finished blending. Transfer to a jar and let cool before screwing the lid on. This will keep in the fridge for 2 to 3 months.

Chocolate Hazelnut Butter

YIELD: 1 CUP (258 G)

Man alive, this recipe is delicious! I often start my mornings with a heaping spoonful of this Chocolate Hazelnut Butter. It tastes like Nutella, except better because you made it yourself!

¾ cup (194 g) Hazelnut Butter (page 120)

¼ cup (50 g) unrefined cane sugar

2 tbsp (11 g) cocoa powder

1 tbsp (15 ml) melted coconut oil

½ tsp sea salt

Add all of the ingredients to your Vitamix and blend until smooth and evenly cocoa-colored. Transfer to a jar and let cool before screwing the lid on. This will keep in the fridge for 2 to 3 months.

Almond Butter

YIELD: 2 CUPS (572 G)

Almond butter is queen! Toasted almonds make a wonderfully creamy butter and have incredible flavor: nutty, naturally a little sweet and super rich. Almond butter is high in healthy fats, protein and fiber. I love pairing almond butter with apples or dark chocolate.

4 cups (572 g) raw almonds

½ tsp sea salt (optional)

Preheat the oven to 350°F (180°C). Line a baking sheet with parchment paper.

Evenly spread the raw almonds on the baking sheet. Bake for 15 to 20 minutes, or until the almonds begin to smell fragrant and appear golden brown. Be cautious and attentive here, because the nuts can quickly burn. Let the almonds cool, and then remove as much of their skins as possible. This step makes for a creamier almond butter!

Add the cooled almonds to your Vitamix. Blend in 5-minute increments for 10 to 15 minutes, stopping whenever you need to scrape down the sides and give your blender a break so it doesn't overheat. It will take some time, but eventually the almonds will transform into a creamy butter. The longer you blend, the creamier it gets as the oils are released. Add the salt, if using, just before you're finished blending. Transfer to a jar and let cool before screwing the lid on. This will keep in the fridge for 2 to 3 months.

Spiced Almond Butter with Cinnamon and Maca

YIELD: 1 CUP (258 G)

This is inspired by a unique spiced almond butter I tried at a friend's house some years ago. Cinnamon, maca and vanilla turn rich and creamy almond butter into almost a dessert!? The taste of maca (a highly nutritious Peruvian root) isn't for everyone, so if you don't dig it, no sweat. Just leave it out. If you are interested in trying maca out, you can find it online or at your local health food store.

1 cup (258 g) Almond Butter (page 124)

½ tsp cinnamon powder

½ tsp maca powder

½ tsp vanilla extract

2 tbsp (30 g) unrefined cane sugar, plus more to taste

¼ tsp sea salt

Add all of the ingredients to your Vitamix and blend until smooth. Add more sugar, if desired. Transfer to a jar and let cool before screwing the lid on. This will keep in the fridge for 2 to 3 months.

Cashew Butter

YIELD: 2 CUPS (584 G)

Cashews are a mild-tasting nut, and thus work well for adding to other plant-based blender recipes like cheesy sauces or caramels. Cashew butter doesn't make for as creamy a nut butter as almonds or hazelnuts, because cashews are lower in fat. But if you're patient with your Vitamix, you will still end up with a smooth nut butter! I like to add a little virgin coconut oil to my cashew butter to help it blend up. This is a great idea for those of us who like coconut. If you don't like the flavor of coconut, use refined coconut oil.

4 cups (584 g) raw cashews

1–2 tbsp (15–30 ml) melted coconut oil (optional)

½ tsp sea salt (optional)

Preheat the oven to 350°F (180°C). Line a baking sheet with parchment paper.

Evenly spread the raw cashews on the baking sheet. Bake for 15 to 20 minutes, or until the cashews begin to smell fragrant and appear golden brown. Be cautious and attentive here, because the nuts can quickly burn. Let the cashews cool enough so you can handle them.

Add the cooled cashews to your Vitamix. Blend in 5-minute increments for 10 to 15 minutes, stopping whenever you need to scrape down the sides and give your blender a break so it doesn't overheat. It will take some time, but eventually the cashews will transform into a creamy butter. The longer you blend, the creamier it gets as the oils are released. If your cashew butter needs some help getting creamy, add 1 to 2 tablespoons (15 to 30 ml) of the melted coconut oil. Add the salt, if using, just before you're finished blending. Transfer to a jar and let cool before screwing the lid on. This will keep in the fridge for 2 to 3 months.

Caramel Cashew Butter

YIELD: 1½ CUPS (400 G)

This caramel cashew butter makes an excellent topping for ice cream. I also like to have it with crunchy, tart fruits like green apples. Of course, it's always great on its own, too.

1 cup (292 g) Cashew Butter (page 128)

½ cup (120 ml) Salted Date Caramel (page 90)

Add the ingredients to your Vitamix and blend until smooth. Transfer to a glass jar and store in the fridge. This will keep in the fridge for 1 to 2 months. You can also simply swirl the caramel into the cashew butter in a jar.

Coconut Butter

YIELD: 2 CUPS (370 G)

For those of us who adore coconut: Welcome to HEAVEN! I used to spend a lot of money treating myself to jars of artisanal coconut butter . . . until I found out I can make it just as good in my Vitamix. Similar to nut butters, you just need patience to achieve that desired creamy, smooth texture. Coconut is naturally so fatty you actually don't need to toast it before blending. Whether you toast or don't toast is a matter of preference.

4 cups (372 g) raw shredded/desiccated coconut

½ tsp sea salt (optional)

If you want to use toasted coconut, preheat the oven to 350°F (180°C). Line a baking sheet with parchment paper.

Evenly spread the coconut flakes on the baking sheet, and bake for 5 to 10 minutes, or until the coconut begins to smell fragrant and appears golden brown. Be cautious and attentive here, because the coconut can quickly burn. Let the coconut flakes cool. Now continue making your coconut butter following the directions below.

Add the coconut flakes (raw or toasted) to your Vitamix. Blend in 5-minute increments for 5 to 10 minutes, stopping whenever you need to scrape down the sides and give your blender a break so it doesn't overheat. It will take some time, but eventually the coconut will transform into a creamy butter. The longer you blend, the creamier it gets as the oils are released. Add the salt, if using, just before you're finished blending. Transfer to a jar and let cool before screwing the lid on. This will keep in the fridge for 2 to 3 months.

Almond Milk

YIELD: 4 CUPS (960 ML)

The classic non-dairy milk: almond! As long as you don't mind the hands-on time, making your own almond milk is way more affordable AND more delicious compared to store-bought varieties. There is nothing like freshly made almond milk. Feel free to play with different flavorings, like vanilla or chai. I offer a chocolate almond milk recipe on page 136.

1 cup (143 g) raw almonds, soaked in water overnight and rinsed

4 cups (960 ml) cold water

Pinch of sea salt

Drain and rinse the soaked almonds, discarding the water they soaked in (or use it to water your plants!) Add the rinsed almonds, fresh water and salt to your Vitamix, and blend for 1 to 2 minutes, or until you have almond milk in your blender! Strain the almond milk using a nut milk bag, cheesecloth or fine sieve. Store in airtight glassware in the fridge for up to 7 days.

Chocolate Almond Milk

YIELD: 2 CUPS (480 ML)

Chocolate milk is a nostalgic drink for me. I used to love when it was included in my school lunches as a kid. So whenever I have it now, I am transported back to a more innocent and simpler time. A round of applause for foods that reconnect you to your inner child!

2 cups (480 ml) Almond Milk (page 135)

2 tbsp (11 g) cocoa powder

1 tbsp (15 ml) maple syrup, plus more to taste

½ tsp vanilla extract

Add all of the ingredients to your Vitamix and blend until smooth, adding more maple syrup, if desired. I am *assuming* you'll be drinking this right away because it's irresistible, but it will keep in airtight glassware in the fridge for up to 7 days.

Oat Milk

Oat milk is my favorite type of non-dairy milk. It's creamy, naturally on the sweeter side and is subtler in flavor than nut milks. Oat milk is trendy at the moment, so it can be pricey in stores. But when you make it yourself in your Vitamix, it's actually one of the cheapest plant milk options, since rolled oats are so inexpensive. It's also quicker to make oat milk than nut milk because you don't have to soak the oats. The only tricky part about oat milk is that it can get slimy if you don't follow a few tried-and-true tips. First: Use ice-cold water. We are not trying to make oatmeal here, people! Second: Don't over-blend. Third: Strain with a very fine-mesh nut milk bag, and consider straining twice if you want it super smooth.

1 cup (90 g) gluten-free rolled oats

4 cups (960 ml) cold water

Pinch of sea salt

Add all of the ingredients to your Vitamix and blend for 20 to 30 seconds. Strain through a fine-mesh nut milk bag. Strain a second time if you want your oat milk extra-smooth. Store in airtight glassware in the fridge for up to 7 days.

Spiced Oat Milk

YIELD: 2 CUPS (480 ML)

This is a delightful take on masala chai (aka spiced tea), made with oat milk,
maple syrup and a splash of vanilla.

2 cups (480 ml) Oat Milk
(page 139)

1 tsp masala chai blend*

½ tsp vanilla extract

1 tbsp (15 ml) maple syrup, plus
more to taste

*Masala chai blends typically
include cinnamon, cardamom,
star anise, black pepper, ginger,
allspice, cloves, fennel and
nutmeg.

Add all of the ingredients to your Vitamix and blend until smooth. Add
more maple syrup, if desired. Serve right away warm or cold, or store in
airtight glassware in the fridge for up to 7 days.

Cultured Coconut Yogurt

YIELD: 1¾ CUPS (450 ML)

This recipe is rich, creamy and delicious. Perfect with berries, granola and a drizzle of maple syrup. You will need some patience to let the yogurt culture, but the result is dreamy!

1 (13.5-oz [398-ml]) can full-fat coconut milk

1 tbsp (15 ml) maple syrup

2 tbsp (30 ml) lemon juice

1 tbsp (8 g) gluten-free cornstarch

4 vegan, gluten-free probiotic capsules

Heat the coconut milk in a microwave or on the stovetop until it's steaming. Add the milk, maple syrup and lemon juice to your Vitamix, and blend for a few seconds until evenly combined. Let it sit for 1 minute. Add the cornstarch and blend for 1 minute. Let it sit for 1 minute, and then blend for 1 more minute. Pour the mixture into a glass container and let it cool for 30 minutes. Stir in the probiotic capsules with a clean wooden spoon. Cover the container with cheesecloth and let it sit in your unheated oven with the light on for 6 to 8 hours to culture. When it begins to smell like yogurt, it's ready. Keep it in the fridge for 1 to 2 days before eating so it thickens, and voilà! You should have rich, tangy, creamy coconut yogurt with all the benefits of the probiotics. You may need to whisk the yogurt after refrigeration to recombine the fats with the water. This will keep in the fridge for 2 to 3 weeks.

Hemp Seed and Almond Rosemary Crackers

YIELD: 25-40 CRACKERS, DEPENDING ON SIZE

Making your own crackers feels so fancy to me, and it always sounds impressive when you can tell your houseguests or friends that these delicious crackers are not store-bought, but handmade! You can technically make these totally by hand without a Vitamix, but it speeds things along. I enjoy these crackers with almost anything, even on their own. They offer a fair amount of protein thanks to the chickpea flour and hemp seeds, and lots of fiber from all the nuts and seeds. Their flavor is delicate and savory with just a hint of rosemary, so they pair well with many different toppings, especially tart ones like cheeses and fermented fruits and vegetables.

2 cups (224 g) almond flour

2 tbsp (14 g) ground flaxseed

2 tbsp (10 g) nutritional yeast flakes

1 tsp garlic powder

1 tsp sea salt

½ tsp onion powder

½ tsp dried ground rosemary

¼ tsp cracked black pepper

¼ cup (60 ml) extra-virgin olive oil

2 tbsp (30 ml) lemon juice

½ cup (80 g) hemp seeds

Preheat the oven to 350°F (180°C). Line a baking sheet with parchment paper.

Add all the dry ingredients, *except* the hemp seeds, to your Vitamix, and blend for 5 seconds, or until all the dry ingredients are evenly mixed. Add the wet ingredients and blend for 10 seconds, or until you have a thick, wet mixture that you can mold with your hands. Scoop into a bowl and add the hemp seeds by hand.

Scoop all the cracker dough onto the baking sheet, and then add another piece of parchment paper on top. Roll the cracker dough out between the two pieces of parchment paper until it's evenly ⅕ inch (5 mm) thick. Score with a knife or pizza cutter into whatever shapes you like. (You could even make them into circles using the top of a glass.) Just keep them all generally the same size. Bake for 15 minutes, or until the crackers are beginning to brown around their edges. Flip them over and bake for 5 to 10 minutes, or until they are brown on the edges and as crunchy as you prefer. Let them cool for 10 minutes, and then enjoy! These will keep at room temperature or in the fridge for 1 week.

Savory Gluten-Free Tart Crust

YIELD: 1 (9" [23-CM]) CRUST

I always like to add something extra to my dough, so to make this basic tart crust special, we're throwing in black pepper, garlic and herbs. I use this crust for my Tofu Quiche with Mushrooms, Spinach and Leek recipe (page 51), but you can fill it with whatever you like! I recommend using a metal tart pan with a removable bottom.

1½ cups (188 g) gluten-free all-purpose flour blend

½ cup (45 g) gluten-free rolled oats

¼ tsp cracked black pepper

½ tsp garlic powder

1 tsp gluten-free cornstarch

½ tsp fresh rosemary leaves

½ tsp fresh thyme leaves

1 tbsp (7 g) ground flaxseeds mixed with 3 tbsp (45 ml) water

3 tbsp (45 ml) extra-virgin olive oil

¼ cup (60 ml) cold water, or more as needed

Preheat the oven to 350°F (180°C). Line the bottom of a 9-inch (23-cm) tart pan with parchment paper, or grease it with non-dairy margarine or vegetable oil.

Add the flour, oats, pepper, garlic powder and cornstarch to your Vitamix. Blend for 5 seconds, or until everything is evenly mixed. Add the remaining ingredients, and blend for 5 to 10 seconds. Scoop this into a bowl and finish by hand. Add more water as needed and knead until you get a thick, pliable dough that sticks together when you press it between your fingers. Scoop your dough into the pan and evenly press it on the bottom and sides, keeping it less than ½ inch (1.3 cm) thick. Poke several holes in the bottom of the crust with a fork. Bake for 10 minutes. We don't want to bake the crust completely right now, because it will be going back in the oven for whatever recipe you're filling it with.

Acknowledgments and Thank Yous

Thank you, Mother Earth, for providing all the energy and resources needed to get this book completed! What an honor to be alive!

Thank you, Page Street Publishing (looking at you, Marissa!), for trusting me once again to write a cookbook and for getting it distributed all over the globe. Endless gratitude to designers Laura, Meg and many others, for making this cookbook look great. Big thanks to copy editor Joe for making all the nitty-gritty details airtight.

Thank you Fable for the beautiful, artisan-crafted dishes I photographed many of these recipes on. Find them at @dinewithfable on the web!

Thank you to my friends, family and girlfriend for eating all these recipes.

Thank YOU, reader, for supporting my work and trying out these recipes. I love to hear from you, so if you ever have any comments, questions, or if you simply feel like saying hey, drop me a line at emilyvoneuw@gmail.com or message me on Instagram at @thisrawsomeveganlife!

About the Author

Emily von Euw (pronouns: they/them/their) is the creator of the award-winning recipe blog This Rawsome Vegan Life (thisrawsomeveganlife.com) and the author of multiple internationally published cookbooks, including the bestselling *Rawsome Vegan Baking*. Em's passion in life comes from food, friendships, wilderness adventures, mindfulness, art and lots of dark chocolate. They have presented at veg expos and festivals across Canada and the U.S., and their work has been featured in publications around the world, including *O, the Oprah Magazine* and VegNews. Em lives with their amazing girlfriend on Vancouver Island, Canada, on land belonging to the Snuneymuxw First Nation.

Website: www.thisrawsomeveganlife.com
Instagram and Facebook: @thisrawsomeveganlife
Twitter: @rawsomevegan
Pinterest: This Rawsome Vegan Life

Index